The Return of the Saints

Their journey home to Gorton

Monastery Publications

Beggars and Builders
by Tony Hurley

Assisi to Gorton
by Fr. Agnellus Andrew

Gorton Monastery, 1861-1961
by Fr. Justin McLoughlin

The Greyfriars Players, 1937-1948
by Fr. Agnellus Andrew

The Return of the Saints

Their journey home to Gorton.

Edited by
Janet Wallwork

Photography by
Graham North

Second Edition

Monastery Publications

The Return of the Saints: their journey home to Gorton by Janet Wallwork, published by Monastery Publications, Manchester, 2012.
Second edition, 2014

ISBN 978-0-9571484-4-4

Printed in Great Britain by Book Printing UK, Remus House, Coltsfoot Drive, Woodston, Peterborough PE2 9BF

Cover design by Imagine: Graphic Designers, The Stables, Paradise Wharf, Ducie Street, Manchester M1 2JN

All proceeds from the sale of this book will go to
The Monastery of St. Francis and Gorton Trust,
Gorton Lane, Manchester, M12 5WF
Registered Charity No. 1061457

www.themonastery.co.uk

Dedication

to all *our* Saints and Angels –
The Monastery's Friends, Volunteers and all who have worked
to bring about
The Return of the Saints.

COMMENT

Manchester EveningNews

Saints 'n' winners

MANCHESTER has had a knack in recent years of finding new uses, new relevance for the relics of the past. Gorton Monastery is a marvellous example of that. Surplus to the requirements of the Franciscan monks who built it, this gem of a building mouldered for years, victim to weather and vandalism, until the dedication of certain individuals and the availability of grants allowed it to be reborn as a modern events venue.

The most affecting aspect of the monastery's story was that of the statues of the saints. Removed at a time when a property developer planned to turn the building into flats, the statues came close to being sold at auction. Objections were raised, the sale was stopped and the statues rescued by Manchester city council. Today we report the return of the saints to their proper place in the monastery. One does not need to be religious to feel a debt to history has been repaid, and Manchester's cultural heritage is a little richer for this.

Manchester Evening News: 9th September, 2011

Contents

Foreword

In the very early days of the Trust, some 16 years ago, we started our search for the missing treasures that had been taken from the building after the Franciscans left and the church had closed.

We were heartened to hear of the story of the rescue of the twelve Gorton saints. We were even more relieved to know that they were being safely held in a storage container in a Manchester City Council depot, in the hope that one day they could be restored and returned to their rightful places on the plinths high above the nave in the Monastery.

Of course there wasn't much point in campaigning and fundraising for the restoration and return of the saints while the Monastery lay in ruins following years of neglect and vandalism. Our priority had to be saving the building and in time we hoped we would be successful in raising the millions that would be needed to do that. One day soon I hope that I will be able to find the time to write that story, but until then you can find a summary of the Trust's 'Story So Far' near the end of this book and find more information about the project in our other DVDs and Monastery publications.

As the Monastery project has unfolded over the years there have been some very unusual and uncanny coincidences relating to the timing of certain major events and around many of the decisions and important dates. There have also been times when the project was facing hardship and failure when someone, something or some important information turned up just in the nick of time. It always seemed to be at the eleventh hour, and it always tested our faith and commitment to the limit, but the solutions to everything always seem to have been magically found in the end.

In many cases, but not always, this magic helped us to get the money we needed to carry on with the project and our campaign to save the Monastery. As you will read in the pages that follow, this Monastery Magic has been at work during our 'Save the Saints' campaign.

We are so thrilled to see our beloved Franciscan saints glowing with newly restored pride back where they belong after more than 20 years since their removal. It has been a significant and extremely moving project for all who have been involved in the process. It has been a once in a lifetime experience that has touched our lives rather more than we had imagined.

The 'Return of the Saints' project would not have been possible without the generosity, hard work and devotion of many, many people. We are indebted to each and every one of you - and we simply could not have achieved this without you.

Many readers will already know that 2012 is a special year and the 150th Anniversary of the Franciscan community in Gorton. It is also 140 years since the saints were first installed in the nave. It was always the dream of our small voluntary team in the Trust's early days that the saints could be brought home to celebrate this special anniversary.

That dream became even more poignant when we lost our dear friend and colleague Tony Hurley (former Trustee, Historian & Tour Guide) after a short battle with cancer early in 2011. Our resolve and determination increased even more with the sudden loss of Audrey Bradshaw (Trust Administrator and Manager of the Angels Community Building) at the beginning of 2012.

The 'Return of the Saints' project was going to be Tony's responsibility and Audrey had always been the one who kept a close eye on them for over a decade while they were in storage. It seemed even more important that we carried on with the project in their memory. We felt that 2011 had to be the year they were brought back home on site to Gorton so at last they could be restored – and 2012 had to be the year when they would be put back where they belong. However, there was one major drawback – we had no funds to pay for the project.

We decided that the best way to raise the money that was needed for the Saints restoration was through sponsorship and we would also host a very special fundraising 'Saints Supper'. It would also be an evening of celebration when we could thank everyone who has played their part in the Monastery's success since the Trust was formed.

A date for the 'Saints Supper' was agreed and we started to plan the evening and invite the VIP guests when we realised that it would be on Midsummer Night -Thursday the 21st June 2012. Uncannily this date would be exactly 5 years to the day when we held the first ever event in the newly restored building back in June 2007.

Do I detect the saints actually smiling down on all of us right now? Is it just another coincidence...or a little bit of Monastery Magic, I wonder?

Rather than create a souvenir brochure for the 'Saints Supper', we decided to publish this book instead as a more permanent record of this important milestone in the history of the project. It has been made possible by the hard work and dedication of Janet Wallwork, David Ratcliffe and Graham North in a remarkably short space of time.

Thank you to everyone for your continued support of the Monastery project and our charitable work in the local community.

Elaine Griffiths MBE
Chief Executive
The Monastery of St. Francis & Gorton Trust

June 2012

Chapter One

Rescue

'On Wednesday, Sotheby's Sussex caters for religious enthusiasts at its garden statuary sale, with an imposing set of 12 sandstone figures of saints dating from the last century. Recently removed from Gorton Friary, near Manchester, each 6ft figure is estimated at £1,000 to £2,000.'

The Times, 17th September, 1994

One Saturday morning, back in 1994, I opened my newspaper and my attention was caught by a striking photo of half a dozen life-size stone statues, obviously of Saints. I immediately realized that one was the figure of Saint Elizabeth of Hungary - one of the most easily recognized saints as she is always depicted as a crowned Queen, holding out an apron full of roses. Alongside were other distinctive saints such as Saint Bonaventure (holding the large hat of a Cardinal) and Saint Anthony (holding the Christ Child and a book) and I suddenly realized that they were all Franciscans, and that they matched the statues from the Gorton Monastery building, which had closed in 1989.

The photo belonged to the weekly round-up of forthcoming auctions, and sure enough, the text stated that the statues were from 'Gorton Friary' – which was the correct name of the church, though generations of local people always referred to it as 'Gorton Monastery'.

The Times, 17th September, 1994

I was greatly concerned when I read this. When the church was open, and run by friars of the Franciscan Order, I had been a member of the Third Order of Saint Francis – an organization of lay people who were inspired by Saint Francis of Assisi and who associated themselves with, and supported, Franciscan communities. Once a month the local group met at Gorton Monastery, and so I had grown to know these statues well. When the Franciscan Order regretfully withdrew from Gorton, at the end of 1989, the church and friary buildings were sold to a developer, who planned to turn them into flats. This had proved impossible – the buildings were Grade 2 listed, and eventually the developer went bankrupt and the church and friary were left standing empty. The buildings were repeatedly plundered and vandalised whilst their ultimate fate remained uncertain.

I was quite sure that the statues should not have been removed, however – they were part of the original architect's design for the church, and should have been protected by its listed status. It so happened that I work at the John Rylands University Library, which often had dealings with Sotheby's, and so I knew the name of the then director, Michael Thomson-Glover. I rang him straight away, that Saturday morning, and fortunately was put straight through (perhaps his staff thought I wished to buy or sell some books!) I

14

explained my concerns and he assured me that his staff would have checked the status of the statues carefully before listing them for sale, but he promised that someone would get back to me.

On 21st September I received a letter from the manager of the 'Garden Statuary Department' at Sotheby's, stating that the vendor had purchased the statues from the development company, and had the 'necessary permission' to remove them, and so they were confident that the sale could go ahead. In fact the catalogue revealed that they were also selling the large crucifix, which had hung from the roof of the church, above the Sanctuary. They did also send me a copy of the catalogue, just in case I wanted to go and bid for them! The sale was to take place on 28th September, so I knew I had just one week to save the saints.

The immediate problem was that I had no idea which organisation was responsible for protecting listed buildings. Fortunately, working in the University of Manchester, I knew that many University buildings were listed and a quick phone call to our Estates Department gave me the information that it was the job of the local authority. They also gave me the name and number of their usual contact at Manchester City Council.

The news when I rang was initially good – it confirmed that the statues should not have been removed. The developer had only been given permission to move them into the new entrance foyer of the converted building, which was proposed for the Sanctuary area, where the High Altar stood. However, the person I spoke to had then to go and 'take advice' about how to deal with this. When they rang back they said that, with regret, the Council did not feel able to take any action. Firstly, they felt the crucifix was not part of the original design, and had no listing protection. And though the statues should not have been removed, any attempt to have the sale stopped could result in legal action by the vendor or by Sotheby's, and losing the case could cost the Council a great deal of money in fees and damages.

I felt that the only way to put pressure on the Council was to show that this issue was important to lots of people, not just to me. Initially I tried to contact my local Councillors, but unfortunately they were attending their national Party Conference, and couldn't be reached. The same was true, initially, of my local M.P., Gerald (now Sir Gerald) Kaufman.

I could see that the only way was to enlist public support, and so my next strategy was to approach the media. I tracked down contacts for all the local, national and religious papers, magazines and local TV channels that I could think of. Wherever there was the slightest interest I posted or hand-delivered them more information. They, in turn, started ringing the Council to see what was going on, and checking if they had really refused to act. Once the story appeared in the press and on television, concerned members of the public started contacting the Council and the press, to protest against the sale.

By now my message had reached our M.P., Gerald Kaufman. He had recently become Chair of the Select Committee on National Heritage, and was understandably keen to defend an endangered piece of that National Heritage that was located in his own constituency; he promised to join in by putting pressure on Council officials to intervene, even ringing the Leader of the Council at home on a Sunday morning.

'Sin' cry as saints are marched into auction

A DOZEN historic statues from one of Manchester's most important church buildings were under threat of being sold off as garden ornaments today.

But an 11th-hour appeal to Sotheby's legal department was being made by Manchester's chief planning officer Dr Ted Kitchen.

The council claims the statues of various saints, removed from St Francis church and friary in Gorton, were protected by the friary's status as a listed building.

The 6ft-high figures were supposed to take pride of place in a scheme to convert the building to luxury flats, officers said.

Just hours before the auction in West Sussex, Dr Kitchen faxed a letter to Sotheby's warning that if the sale went ahead police would be asked to investigate because "somewhere in the chain of events, something illegal must have happened."

But Sotheby's said the sale would go ahead unless the council could show the statues were specifically included in documentation relating to St Francis's listing.

The fuss began when an astonished member of the public saw an auction catalogue and realised these important bits of the building — which is awaiting £5m conversion work — were up for sale.

St Francis — designed by Edward Pugin, son of the architect of the Houses of Parliament — has been at the centre of controversy since its sale by the Franciscan Order.

Grants worth over £800,000 were awarded to Nottingham-based developers Zodeco Homes, but the conversion work has yet to start three and a half years after planning permission was granted.

Zodeco Homes went into liquidation, but developer Charles Zodeh had hoped to revive the plan through a sister company European Homes.

In the meantime, vandals have caused thousands of pounds of damage.

Mr Zodeh could not be contacted for a comment.

The 130-year-old sandstone statues, whose reserve prices at auction were up to £2,000 each, were set in arches in the church.

Council conservation officer Brian Wilson said there had been an unwritten agreement with the developers that the statues would be removed during the renovation, then re-sited near the old altar to create a spectacular display area.

Alarm bells rang when librarian Janet Wallwork, a former secretary of an order for lay people at St Francis, saw the statues in an auction supplement.

EXCLUSIVE

By Paul Taylor

"I spoke to Sotheby's in West Sussex and it seemed the statues were being sold as garden ornaments," she said.

James Rylands, director of garden statuary at Sotheby's, said the statues had been brought to them by a bona fide vendor who had a receipt for their purchase from European Homes in August 1993.

Sotheby's temporarily withdrew them for sale after objections from the city council, but decided to go ahead after, Mr Rylands claimed, the city council could not produce documentary evidence that the statues were part of the building's listing.

"Sotheby's do not sell anything where there is any doubt over the legality of selling it," he said. "But there does not seem to be any doubt about the legality of the sale."

But today Dr Kitchen said: "He has got the law wrong."

Robin Bluhm of Manchester's Victorian Society said: "St Francis holds a very high place among the surviving ecclesiastical places in Manchester. Any spoliation of it is a matter for grave alarm."

And a spokesman for the Franciscan Order said he was "very sad" to hear the saints may be sold off.

Manchester Evening News, 28th September, 1994,

Meanwhile, Manchester's Chief Planning officer, Dr Ted Kitchen, had rung Sotheby's and asked that they withdraw the statues temporarily from sale. Unfortunately, after initially agreeing, they then changed their minds, as they claimed the Council had failed to demonstrate that the statues were integral to the building, and they proposed to re-list them. By this time, however, I had had time to do some research, and could produce references from two books on the history of the Monastery, proving that they were designed by one of the founder members of the community – Father Cuthbert Wood, and were part of the original designs of the architect – the famous Edward Welby Pugin. In fact such a collection of 12 life size statues of Franciscan Saints is certainly extremely rare, and possibly unique.

Catholic Times. 2nd October, 1994,

I passed information on to Dr Kitchen, who contacted Sotheby's again, mentioning the new information he had, and pointing out the possibility of the Council taking legal action and thus generating bad publicity. Reluctantly Sotheby's agreed to another temporary withdrawal whilst the council put a case together.

Meanwhile the protests about the sale grew, since I was encouraging as many people as I could - local residents, historians and religious individuals to show that they opposed the sale. For five years local people had watched helplessly as items had been taken out of the church whilst it stood empty: even the lead had been stripped from the Friary roof. Unfortunately, the police had been powerless as they could never catch anyone in the act. Here, at last, there seemed to be a chance to get something back, and people responded enthusiastically to that opportunity.

The Council took legal advice, as well as consulting the Victorian Society, the Civic Society and English Heritage. Over the next three months the statues were in a state of limbo, whilst the Council engaged in discussions about what to do. Since the developer's scheme was defunct the statues could not be returned to the empty building, which was suffering constant break-ins. The only positive news was that a company called G.A.P. Developments had started negotiations with Grant Thornton (who had been appointed as Official Receivers for the bankrupt developer), with the intention of acquiring the buildings and converting them into affordable housing.

I kept the pressure up, of course, and in December Ted sent me a copy of a proposal he was putting to the Council's Environmental Planning Committee, that was to be debated on 5th January 1995. This entailed the Council buying the statues from the vendor, funded by G.A.P., although the cost should later be deducted from the sum G.A.P. already owed the Council for making the site weatherproof. The Council would look after the statues and, ultimately, they would be displayed in a publicly accessible part of the G.A.P. development.

At a meeting on 5th January, 1995, the proposal was agreed, but although the costings of the scheme were discussed, the minutes of this debate were not made publicly available. Unfortunately, there later proved to be insurmountable problems with the development proposal, and it did not proceed. The term granted for negotiation was about to expire when, in April, Sotheby's threatened to list the statues again. However, Ted Kitchen managed to persuade the Council to put up the money and trust that the statues could be saved, and eventually returned.

21

On 25th April a deal was finally agreed by all parties and Manchester City Council became owner of the statues. (The Manchester Evening News reported that £23,000 was to be paid for the statues, though this was never officially confirmed.)

Manchester Evening News, 26th April, 1995.

The next day, Wednesday April 26th, the statues came back to Manchester on the back of a lorry. Initially they were displayed in the Sculpture Hall of the Town Hall, but their fragile condition deteriorated even further, as they stood, unprotected, at ground level. Staff reported that they were constantly being patted, rubbed, kicked – and, once, even spat upon. I protested about this, and a decision was taken to remove them into secure storage, and there they remained for 16 years, locked away in the dark, and largely forgotten, until their return to the Monastery on 8th September, 2011.

The statues on display in Manchester Town Hall.

The statues in the container in the Hooper Street yard.

The statues stored in their container: a picture by the internationally renowned artist, architect, and photographer Dan Dubowitz.

Janet Wallwork
June 2012

Chapter Two

Revelation

The year after the statues went into storage, in 1996, the Monastery of St. Francis and Gorton Trust was established by Elaine and Paul Griffiths. As a child, Paul had been an altar boy at the Church, and had been appalled when he saw the condition into which it had deteriorated. He and his wife Elaine established a charitable trust to save the buildings, and find them a new role in the heart of the local community. I joined the Trust in its early stages, and one of our earliest tasks was researching the history of the buildings, and their contents, to support our funding bids.

Much had been lost, damaged or destroyed in the years the Church had stood empty. However, one task to which all were committed was that somehow, at some future stage when the buildings were secure, the statues – and perhaps even the crucifix – should be brought back.[1]

It was, therefore, necessary to try and research the history of the statues, and to identify the saints they represented. Although books confirmed they were of Franciscan saints, the only clear images that we had were from the Sotheby's catalogue. The original statues were now stored securely, but were inaccessible, though it was clear from the auction photos that they had suffered considerable damage.

---

[1] The story of the return of the crucifix is told in *Beggars and Builders: My Story of Gorton Monastery* by Tony Hurley. (Monastery Publications: Manchester, 2012.)

The statues after they were removed from the church, waiting to be sent down to Sotheby's

The first task was identification. The statues were designed by a member of the Community, Father Cuthbert Wood, however none of his notes or drawings survived. They were made by a Manchester company, William Wilson & Co. Unfortunately they went bankrupt in the early years of the 20th century, and their records and archives have not survived either. It seemed our only option was to study the appearance of the statues for clues to their identity.

Wilson William & Co. wholesale, retail and export ironmongers, marble masons and gas fitters, manufacturers of marble chimney pieces, washstands, monuments, &c. register and other grates, kitchen ranges, and general gas and steam cooking apparatus, stable fittings, gates and railings, cast iron baths, garden chairs, tables, vases and fountains, lawn mowers and rollers, gas chandeliers, hall lamps and brackets, iron and brass bedsteads, electro-plated ware, cutlery, builders' ironmongers, &c. contractors for the heating by hot water, steam, and hot air, for the lighting by gas, for the cooking and other culinary arrangements in public institutions, hotels, &c. patentees of Wilson & Co.'s patent hot-water cylinder for the prevention of boiler explosions, 50 King st. 49 South King st. and 3 and 5 St. James's square; marble works, 1 St. James's square

William Wilson's entry from *Slater's Directory of Manchester and Salford*, 1877-8.

There is an established iconography of the images of saints, which would have been well-known to people in medieval times. They may not have been able to read, but if they saw a statue or a painting or a picture in stained glass, they would usually recognise the saint by their 'attributes', which were usually articles and symbols that related to their lives or deaths. Thus Saint Peter would usually carry keys, Saint Christopher would hold the Christ Child, and Saint Catherine would be accompanied by a wheel. Much of this symbolism is now a mystery to all but art historians, though some popular saints remain easy to identify. The saints from the Monastery, though, were much more of a challenge. The parish was founded by Belgian Franciscans, and they chose saints who were important to them, but not necessarily well known in Britain. In fact it is probable that generations of Gortonians sat in the church oblivious to the identities of many of the Saints who watched over them.

Another issue that immediately presented itself was working out which position each had originally occupied in the church. We knew that six saints stood high up on each side of the nave, because their plinths remained. Photographs of the church, however, tended to focus on the sanctuary, and though one could see the three saints that were closest to the altar on each side, the locations of the other six were much harder to work out.

Unfortunately the six statues close to the altar were the ones whose appearance was most distinctive, and thus were easy to identify. For example, Saint Anthony of Padua, one of the best known saints in the Church, almost always appears holding a lily, a book, and the Christ Child. Facing him, Saint Clare of Assisi, the first female follower of Saint Francis, stood dressed as a nun and holding a monstrance.[2] The patron saints of the Franciscan Third Order[3] Saint Louis, King of France and Saint Elizabeth, Queen of Hungary, were easily identified by their crowns and rich clothing. Saint Bonaventure was a cardinal, and so held his huge cardinal's hat. Saint Louis of Toulouse was a bishop, and was dressed in rich robes and wore a mitre on his head. The statues of friars in plain Franciscan habits, were much more of a challenge.

Identifying the saints was made a little easier, however, by the fact that the plinths on which they stood were supported by carvings of angels, holding items relating to the saints and their lives. Nevertheless, the remaining six took considerable effort to identify, and, despite the expert help of the Poor Clare nuns of Hawarden, in Wales, our initial list (appearing in some of our early publications) had three incorrect identifications. This is no reflection on anyone's research skills, however. Part of the problem was that some statues had lost their 'attributes', and the other was that the original designer of the statues, Father Cuthbert, made errors in the details of their appearance.

---

[2] A monstrance is the elaborate vessel which is used to display the Blessed Sacrament for veneration.

[3] Saint Francis established an Order of Friars and one of nuns (now known as the Poor Clares) and they were known as his First and Second Orders. However, many lay people also wanted to follow his teachings, without actually entering religious life. He therefore founded a Third Order for them, so they could still marry, work, and remain living in the community, whilst associating themselves with his philosophy, and supporting the First and Second Orders.

Father Cuthbert

Although he was obviously a great scholar, he was clearly hampered by lack of information on the appearance of the less well-known saints. In the 1860s there were no internet resources, of course, nor was there any major public library for him to visit. Thus, the face of one statue bears a remarkable resemblance to Michelangelo's statue of 'David', no doubt copied from a popular book on art. One statue, dressed as a priest in rochet and biretta, closely resembled pictures of Saint Charles Borromeo. I had read that Saint Charles was a Franciscan tertiary, and so it seemed likely the statue was of him. However, a couple of years ago, the *Manchester Guardian* newspaper published in digital form, and at last one could search for articles about the Monastery. In one of these we found an account of the opening of the church – complete with a list of the statues. The one we had identified as the sixteenth century Charles Borromeo was actually intended to be Saint Ivo (or Ivio) of Brittany – a saint who lived in the thirteenth century, and would have dressed very differently. Presumably Father Cuthbert had no idea of how a thirteenth century priest would dress, and used his imagination. Two other statues had originally been wrongly identified, again because they did not match the usual appearance of those particular saints. Thanks to the *Manchester Guardian*, we now had their identities confirmed, and could start to research their lives.

THE MANCHESTER GUARDIAN

25ᵗʰ September 1872

The Nave is divided into six bays, and over each massive column, in the sprandrel of the arch, is, or is to be, fixed a statue of one of the principal saints of the order. These statues will when completed be twelve in number, six on each side, all life size; and each corbel angel will hold some emblem of the saint above it.

The whole of the carving – which, even to the minutest figure, is symbolical – has been designed by one of the resident fathers, Father Cuthbert.

The following are the twelve saints whose statues will ultimately find a place in the church as described:-

On the north or gospel side:

1, St. Anthony of Padua. This saint having been one of the principal defenders of the Blessed Sacrament, the angel underneath holds a ciborum.

2, St. Bonaventura, a doctor of the Church. The angel holds a scroll and pen.

3, St. Bernadin of Sienna. As this saint was a great preacher of devotion to the Holy Name, the angel holds an exact copy of the monogram which he caused to be painted on the facades of the houses.

4, St. Louis of France, patron of the brothers of the third order. The angel holds a book, expanded, bearing the inscription. "Reg. III. Ord. S.P.N. Francisca." 5, St.Peter of Alcantara. This having angel holds the "discipline." having been a saint of great penance.

6, St. Ivio of Brittany, patron of the secular clergy, tertiaries. The angel holds the cord of St. Francis of the third

order On the south or epistle side are the following:-

1, St. Clare of Assisi. The statue of this saint, and that of St. Anthony of Padua, are placed nearest to the chancel – a place of honour, on account of those saints having been great defenders of the Blessed Sacrament. The angel of St. Clare holds wheat and grapes.

2, St. Louis of Toulouse. This saint renounced his regal dignity, became a Franciscan, and subsequently Bishop of Toulouse. The angel consequently holds a crown.

3, St. Berard, first martyr of the order of St. Francis. The angel holds a Turkish scimitar, symbolical of the martyr's death.

4, St. Elizabeth, Queen of Hungary, patron of the sisters of the third order. The angel holds a shield with a triple crown, emblematic of virginity, married life, and widowhood.

5, St. Leonard of Port Maurice. This saint having been a great preacher of the passion of our Lord, the nagel holds a crown of thorns and three nails.

6, St. Didacus, patron of the lay brothers of the Order of St. Francis. It is said that during the lifetime of this saint, when people flocked to the convent believing in his power to work miracles, he brought the sufferers before the altar, dipped his finger in oil, and made upon them the sign of the cross, telling them that it was by the power of Jesus alone they were healed. The angel, therefore, carries a burning lamp. The whole of the statues are gifts. Five only are as yet in the places prepared for them.

One detail about the statues, which came to light only when this book was in the final stages of preparation, concerns the decoration underneath each plinth. It was always clear that there were flowers carved underneath each statue, but only with the production of really clear and detailed photographs did we realise that each carved group was unique. A message came to us that our former Historical Director, the late Tony Hurley, had a theory that the flowers related directly to the saint above, and he had even suggested a few identifications. In the Victorian era there were many books written about 'The Language of Flowers' and great significance was attached to their appearance in paintings and on jewellery, though this usually contained a romantic message. Far less well-known was that there was a religious significance to various flowers, dating back to the Middle Ages. It would seem this may have been in Father Cuthbert's mind when he designed the statues.

With little time to spare I contacted our friends in the Poor Clare Colettine community of Tŷ Mam Duw, at Hawarden, North Wales, who had helped with the original identification of the saints. As an enclosed community they were unable to visit the Church, but by sending them photographs they were able to give an opinion on the varieties of the flowers, and suggest their relationship to each saint, and so these, together with a little information gleaned from the internet, have been added to each of the following descriptions.

However, I must stress that this is, in fact, a work in progress. The Trust would be very happy to hear from anyone with alternative ideas about the flowers, and, indeed, of those many other plants and flowers which are carved throughout the church.

The following pages give a few brief details on the life of each saint, and some of the areas of which they are patrons. The dates of their feast days are taken from the current Franciscan Liturgical Calendar for the U.K. Different Religious Orders, and different countries, have their own calendars, and there are sometimes slight changes from year to year.

The Saints

Saint Anthony of Padua

1195-1231

Feast Day - June 13th

Perhaps the best loved and most recognisable of saints, Saint Anthony was an early follower of Saint Francis. Born to a noble family in Lisbon he was both intelligent and pious. He entered the Augustinian order, as they were famed for scholarship, and was ordained a priest. In 1219 he met five friars from the Franciscan order, led by Father Berard, on their way to preach the gospel in Morocco, and was deeply impressed. The following year he saw their bodies brought back to Coimbra – the first martyrs of the new order, and sought permission to become a Franciscan. He became a famous preacher, with special devotion to the Holy Child Jesus and to the Blessed Sacrament. He was also deeply devoted to the poor, and is credited with the power to help people find lost items. Many people believe a prayer to Saint Anthony, together with a promise of money to the poor, is the best way to ensure they locate their lost property.

Patron of the poor and oppressed, the infertile, travellers, sailors, fishermen and of lost items, postal services, and domestic animals.

The statue holds a book, to symbolise love of learning and preaching, and carries the Child Jesus, of Whom he had many visions.

His angel supporter plinth carries a ciborium, to represent his love of the Blessed Sacrament.

The flowers are ears of wheat, representing his love for the Blessed Sacrament, and Spikenard flowers, which were once used in making the oil for the anointing of priests.

36

Saint Berard of Carbio

D.o.b.unknown – 1220
Feast Day - January 16th

Berard was a native of Umbria, and was received into the Franciscan Order by Saint Francis himself. He was an excellent preacher, and had studied Arabic, so Saint Francis sent him, with four companions, to preach to the Moors. They travelled to Spain and preached to the Moors of Seville, and were attacked and later banished. They travelled to Morocco and were banished from there also. They returned and, when they denounced the teachings of Mohammed in the market place they were arrested and taken to the Sultan. They refused to renounce their religion despite torture – they were flogged, and had burning oil and vinegar poured into their wounds, before being rolled in salt. Eventually they were beheaded by the Sultan himself; becoming the first martyrs of the Franciscan Order. Their bodies were ransomed and returned to Coimbra where they were seen by Father Anthony – who had met them on their outward journey. As a result he joined their Order, eventually becoming known as Saint Anthony of Padua

Saint Berard's statue holds a book in his left hand and a palm branch, signifying martyrdom in his right.

The angel under his plinth holds a scimitar, the instrument of his death.

The flowers depict a grapevine, perhaps referring to a Biblical verse about harvesting grapes (Joel 3.13) which can be taken as a reference to martyrdom. They also represent the wine of the Eucharist.

Saint Bernadine of Siena

1380-1444

Feast Day: May 20th

Born into a noble family in a small town near Siena, Bernadine first worked in hospitals, nursing the sick. He later joined the Franciscan Order and was famed for his preaching – large crowds turned out to hear him speak. His particular devotion was to the Holy Name of Jesus. Italy at that time was a collection of warring states, all jealous of their individual identity. Bernadine was so charismatic a preacher that he persuaded many cities to take down their coats of arms from the walls of churches and public buildings and replace them with a board displaying the letters I.H.S. – a transcription of the Greek initials for Jesus Christ. He also used to preach holding before him a board, marked with these letters. He became Vicar-General of the Observant branch of the Franciscans, and reformed and expanded the Order and is considered the foremost Italian missionary of the 15th century.

He is patron of advertising, communications, reformed gamblers and those with throat, lung and chest complaints.

His statue holds the plaque he held whilst preaching.

His supporting angel also holds a board with the letters I.H.S.

The flowers are passion flowers, traditionally representing the Passion of Jesus, a subject about which he often preached.

40

Saint Bonaventure

1221-1274
Feast Day - July 15th

Little is known of his background, except he was born in Bagnoregio, Italy and joined the Friars Minor in 1238. He was sent to study in Paris, alongside Saint Thomas Aquinas. He was a great preacher and scholar, and eventually became Minister General of the Friars Minor. His philosophical writings became famous and the Pope made him first a Bishop, then a Cardinal.

After his death he was given the title Doctor of the Church.

He is patron of scholars, and those with bowel disorders.

His statue holds a book, to represent his love of learning and a cross, for his skill as a preacher. The original cross was lost and a new one has been made to replace it.

His supporting angel holds a scroll, which also represents his love of scholarship.

The flowers are lilies, representing chastity and Solomon's Seal, representing wisdom.

42

Saint Clare of Assisi
1194-1253
Feast Day - August 11th

Clare was born the beautiful and talented daughter of an important Italian Count who owned a palace in Assisi. At the age of 18 she heard Saint Francis preach and resolved, somehow, to follow him. It was arranged that she should leave her family in secret, and Francis arranged temporary shelter for her with some Benedictine nuns. Eventually a simple convent building was obtained where Clare, with her sister Agnes and other like-minded women, founded the Order of Poor Ladies – now known as the Poor Clares. The Order – then and now - focused on 'Holy Poverty' and lived as simply as possible. Clare had a tremendous devotion to the Blessed Sacrament. In 1234 the army of Frederick II attacked the convent and Clare left her sick bed and carried the ciborium holding the Blessed Sacrament to a window where she held it aloft. The soldiers were dazzled and ran away, leaving the convent – and the town of Assisi safe. Thus images of Clare usually show her holding a ciborium or monstrance. On another occasion, when she was sick on Christmas Eve, she very much wished to attend Mass, but was unable to do so. However, on the wall of her cell she was granted a 'real-time' vision of Saint Francis, saying Mass many miles away. She was thus proclaimed patron of television.

Patron of television, telecommunications, eye complaints, needleworkers and goldsmiths.

Her statue originally carried a monstrance, which was badly damaged, but has since been reconstructed.

Her angel supporter holds wheat and grapes, to represent the bread and wine of the Eucharist.

The flowers are roses, meaning love, and either thistles, to signify penance or clover flowers meaning humility (because clover is trodden underfoot).

43

44

Saint Didacus
1400-1463
Feast Day - November 13th

Born into a poor family, Didacus entered the Franciscan Order as a lay brother. His piety, zeal and prudence led to him becoming Superior of a community in the Canary Islands – almost unheard of for a lay Brother. Later he was sent to Rome to attend the canonisation of Saint Bernadine of Siena, after which he was asked to renounce his responsibilities and instead serve the sick as a humble Infirmarian. He used to have the sick brought to the altar of the church where he anointed them with oil, and acquired a reputation as a miracle worker. His final days were spent as a contemplative hermit.

His statue holds a crucifix.

Patron of Franciscan lay Brothers, and of the Philippines.

His angel supporter holds a ciborium, the vessel which carried the Blessed Sacrament, referring to a time when an angel brought Communion to him when he was far away from a church.

The flowers seem to be petunias and cuckoo flowers, which are Spring flowers, and perhaps represent new life. The cuckoo flower is sometimes said to indicate 'ardour'.

46

Saint Elizabeth of Hungary
1207-1231
Feast Day - November 17th.

Elizabeth was born a Princess, the daughter of a King of Hungary. She married the Landgrave (or King) of Thuringia, a German state. She was a religious woman and devoted to acts of charity, supported by her husband. After his death, however, her ungenerous brother-in-law became Regent to her infant son. Elizabeth used to rise very early to take food from the palace kitchens, in secret, to the poor. One morning the Regent caught her and demanded to know what she was doing. She replied that she had come to pick roses. The Regent demanded to see the contents of her apron – whereupon the bread inside it turned into roses. Later she joined the Franciscan Third Order, the lay people who tried to follow Francis. After her death she was declared patron of the women of the Franciscan Third Order.

Patron of charities, hospitals, exiles, the homeless, bakers and lace-makers, and the Franciscan Third Order.

Her statue shows her crowned, with an apron full of roses.

Her angel supporter holds three crowns, to show she had royal status as a virgin, a wife and widow.

The flowers are roses, to represent the miracle for which she is famous, and olives, to signify a fruitful wife.

48

Saint Ivo of Brittany

1253-1303

Feast Day – May 10th

Ivo was born the son of the Lord of Kermartin in Brittany. He was sent to Paris to study Civil Law, then took minor Orders and studied Canon Law. He became an ecclesiastical judge and famous for his incorruptibility. He was known as the advocate and defender of the poor. As a layman he joined the Franciscan Third Order, and was later ordained a priest, and was famed for his preaching.

Patron of lawyers, barristers, judges, abandoned children and Brittany, and of secular Third Order priests.

His statue shows him holding a book, and seems to be dressed (anachronistically) as a 19th century secular priest.

His angel supporter holds the waist-cord of the Third Order.

The flowers are vine leaves, referring to the wine of the Eucharist, and possibly violets representing enclosure, spiritual wisdom and humility.

Saint Leonard of Port Maurice

1676-1751

Feast Day - November 26th

Born the son of a sea captain he gave up a career in medicine to join the Franciscan Order. His health did not permit him to travel abroad as a missionary, but he became a famous preacher all over Italy, preaching devotion to the Blessed Sacrament, Sacred Heart and Immaculate Conception. His greatest feat was establishing devotion to the Way of the Cross, which he set up in over 600 locations including the Colosseum, in Rome. To this day, the Pope still conducts a Way of the Cross procession in the Colosseum every Good Friday.

His statue originally held a raised cross, this was broken, and has now been replaced.

His angel supporter holds a crown of thorns and nails, symbols of the Passion of Jesus.

The flowers are palms, as a reference to Palm Sunday, and either rosehips or hawthorn berries to signify the crown of thorns.

Saint Louis of Toulouse
1274-1297
Feast Day - August 19th

Louis was born a Prince, the second son of the King of Naples. He was also a nephew of Saint Louis, King of France, and great-nephew of Saint Elizabeth, Queen of Hungary. His father was captured by the King of Spain, and his three sons, including Louis, were exchanged for him, as hostages. They were held for seven years and educated by Franciscan friars. Louis resolved to give up his wealth and royal status to become a Franciscan. For political reasons he was made a Bishop, but lived simply, and gave all he could to the poor and hungry.

His statue is dressed as a bishop and originally held a crosier in the right hand, which has had to be replaced.

His angel supporter holds a crown, symbol of his royal birth.

The flowers are blackberry leaves and berries, and as these bear thorns they can signify penitence. They may also refer to a parable in the Bible (Judges 9, 8-15) in which the humble bramble becomes King of all the trees.

54

Saint Louis, King of France
1214-1270
Feast Day – August 25th.

Louis came to the French throne at the age of 11, and is the only King of France to have been canonised. In accordance with the beliefs of those times he joined two Crusades to try and regain control of the Holy Land, and at one point was captured by the Egyptians. When released he spent four years, and much of his wealth, helping the crusaders.

He was also a great patron of the arts, and built the glorious Sainte Chapelle in Paris to house the Crown of Thorns and a fragment of the True Cross – two relics he had brought from the Holy Land. He lived a personal life of austerity and penance, and joined the Franciscan Third Order, whose patron he was later proclaimed.

Patron of prisoners, builders, sculptors, soldiers, hairdressers, and male Franciscan Tertiaries.

His statue is dressed as a King and holds a golden reliquary in the shape of the crown of thorns.

His angel supporter holds a copy of the Rule of the Third Order, in Latin.

The flowers appear to be cinquefoils, and Crown Imperial lilies. The former, also known as *Potentilla*, is a flower depicted in numerous French churches from the 11th century onwards. In heraldry it signifies strength, honour and loyalty. The Crown Imperial lilies signify charity, and could also stand for the royal lilies, the emblems of France.

56

Saint Peter of Alcantara

1499-1562

Feast Day - October 22nd

Born in Spain, son of the Governor of Alcantara, he studied at the University of Salamanca, later joining the Friars of the Strict Observance. He was soon chosen as superior of a Province, and attempted to reform the Order. At first he had little success and became a hermit, but gradually others joined him, and his fame as a preacher and spiritual advisor spread. He knew and influenced Saint John of Avila, Saint Francis Borgia and Saint Teresa of Avila. He slept very little, and promoted night vigils, and Perpetual Adoration of the Blessed Sacrament.

Patron saint of night watchmen, adorers of the Blessed Sacrament and Brazil.

His statue originally held a tall preaching cross, which was lost, though clearly visible on older pictures of the Church. A replacement has now been made.

His angel supporter holds a discipline, or small whip, a symbol of penance.

The flowers seem to be chrysanthemums, a flower often associated with death and funerals, together with wild arum berries (*arum maculatum*). The latter are poisonous, and could represent sin. The wild arum is often known by the traditional name 'Devils and Angels'.

'Where there is darkness, light.'

During the period that the statues were in storage a £6 million restoration programme was taking place in the Monastery and friary buildings. Our Historical Advisor, the late Tony Hurley, was closely involved with supervising that restoration, whilst continuing to research the history of the Monastery. One of his many original discoveries, and perhaps the most significant, initially came about through observation of the unusual lighting effects that had resulted from the church being built on a North-South axis, rather than the more usual East-West. The full, fascinating, story is told in his posthumously-published book, *Beggars and Builders: My Story of Gorton Monastery*. The following extract is reproduced from that book.

Early in 2005, I received a request from some students to film some short pieces of work in the Monastery for their course exam. It was a frosty day with clear blue skies when they arrived, and I accompanied them to the Monastery and stood around for about half an hour. At that time I would normally be taking people around, walking and talking and not standing still for any length of time. The light coming into the Monastery is absolutely amazing and illuminates the building in most beautiful ways. That day was no exception, and by being still in one place I could watch the sunlight move inch by inch across the walls and floors, as the sun rose higher in the sky. It soon became clear that the lights from the high-up thirteen clerestory windows were tracking across the wall towards the positions where statues of Franciscan saints once stood.

As they inched nearer, it became clear that they would indeed line up. As you can see from the next photo, the lights illuminate the position of each saint and strike the midpoint of the arches in between.

It is an awe-inspiring sight and makes your heart sing. Because of the north south alignment, the whole process takes place again in the afternoon, in reverse, on the opposite wall where the other six saints stood. In the eight years we had owned the Monastery, nobody had actually witnessed this event and, to my knowledge, none of the earlier congregation was aware of it. It happens every day when the sun is shining, occurring earlier or later depending on the time of the year.

As you can see, it's a fabulous spectacle. Notice that the lights match the width and height of the saint and pedestals, despite the clerestory windows (above) being taller and wider.

I can't resist a puzzle and began to wonder about the mathematics and geometry involved to achieve such precision.

Also, there are thirteen windows but only twelve 'events' on each wall i.e. saint and arch. Where did the 13th light shine? Was it to do with Fr. Cuthbert's missing crucifix? Was it perhaps a reference to the twelve Apostles and Jesus Christ? '

From **Beggars and Builders: My Story of Gorton Monastery** by Tony Hurley (Monastery Publications: Manchester, 2012) pp 61-3.

This discovery led, initially, to Tony exploring the measurements and layout of the Church, and realising there was an immense significance to every detail of the design – even leading to the discovery of a hidden plan of the church, concealed in the pattern of the tiles in the Sanctuary. It was only when the great crucifix (which had been listed in the same Sotheby's sale as the statues) was returned and re-instated, however, that he was enabled to reveal the most amazing of the secrets of the architect, Edward Pugin. This was that the design and the alignments of the church were so finely calculated and constructed as to ensure that key locations – for example the High Altar, the Lady Chapel, and the statue of Saint Francis, were all lit by the sun on appropriate feast days.

These discoveries all flowed directly from his close observations of the daily illumination of the plinths of the Saints' statues. The return of those statues – an event he had been so longing to see - reminds us how his premature death, in 2011, robbed us of a remarkable and dedicated historian, as well as a wonderful colleague and friend.

Janet Wallwork
June, 2012

Chapter Three

Restoration

After the statues of the saints were returned from Sotheby's, they were displayed at Manchester Town Hall, then in the basement of the Abraham Moss Centre, before being placed in a storage container in a council yard at Hooper Street in Ardwick, Manchester where they remained for about fifteen years. These pictures, taken from the back of the container, show the statues as they are being prepared for transportation back to Gorton Monastery in September 2011. It was obvious that they would need to be cleaned and all the peeling paint removed.

Each of the statues had to be individually wrapped in a thick layer of bubble wrap in order to protect them from further damage during the journey.

These pictures show the statue of Saint Louis of Toulouse bring completely covered, and then strapped up ready to be hoisted into a specially made crate.

The other statues all had to be treated in the same way.

A fork lift truck was used to raise the statues into the crates as they each weighed about half a ton.

The fork lift truck was also used to lift the statues onto a large flat-bed truck. In the interests of safety, no more than four statues were carried on the truck at any one time.

It took two days and four trips to transport all twelve back to the Monastery.

Here a lorry with two statues makes its way slowly along Gorton Lane back towards the Monastery. It had been almost twenty years since the statues were last in Gorton.

Here three more of the statues are being brought back into the Monastery car park.

Above: three of the saints arriving at the Monastery to be unloaded and taken to the new containers for storage until they could be cleaned and repaired.

The picture above shows the statue of St. Leonard being carried from the truck to the container. Once there it would be unwrapped and checked to find out what repairs were needed.

The statues were carried from the truck to the container using this vehicle known as a teli-holder, and then lifted from the crates and placed carefully in the containers. Here, over the next few months they would be restored.

Each container held six of the saints' statues, placed so that all the saints from the west side of the nave were in one container and the ones from the eastern side in the other.

It was now clear how much work needed to be done to restore each of them to their original condition.

Once the twelve statues in the containers had the various paint layers cleaned off, they were ready to have various items repaired or replaced. The square block just visible on the table in the right hand container is the monstrance being carved for St. Clare.

Below, posters were placed on the sides of the containers inviting the public to come and view the saints during restoration: many hundreds of people came to watch as the work progressed.

See the **Saints**
being restored here!

Most Sundays from 12 until 4pm

For details of other Viewing Days and
details on our **'Save a Saint'** campaign
please visit www.themonastery.co.uk   TRUST

Beneath the paint on the statues there was a lot of fine detail, including the motifs and designs shown here on Saint Louis of Toulouse, such as the Fleur de Lys and the lace on his clothing. It only really became visible once the paint was removed.

The saints then began to look as they were intended by their designer, Father Cuthbert Wood.

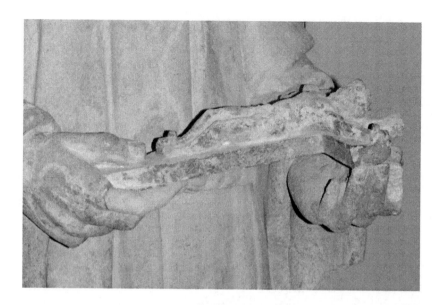

After the paint was carefully removed, minute traces of gilding were discovered on certain statues, for example on the crucifix held by Saint Didacus and the crowns worn by St. Louis, King of France, and St. Elizabeth, Queen of Hungary. It was decided to re-gild all parts of the statues where this evidence was found.

These pictures show the work that was done to the monstrance which St. Clare holds. The original monstrance had been broken and most of the top was missing. Sculptor Andrew Scantlebury carved a new one (inset), and is shown below holding it against the statue. The top two pictures show before and after views of St. Clare. The monstrance was then covered in gold leaf. The face of the statue also needed a considerable amount of restoration.

Shawn Williamson and Andrew Scantlebury at work repairing the saints' statues. They are pictured below with the statue of St. Louis, King of France, the patron saint of sculptors.

The statue of St. Anthony, with the remnants of the white paint peeling off. It was apparent that the figure of the Christ Child had lost its right hand, and the break was covered by the final layer of paint. This proved that it was applied after the statues were removed from the church – perhaps to enhance their saleability as garden ornaments.

The picture below right shows the statue with the paint cleaned off completely, the book with its pages gilded, and Christ's hand restored.

These wooden items were created by two of the Monastery's volunteers to replace lost originals.

The preacher's cross, for St. Peter of Alcantara, below right, was made by Terry Colley, who also applied all of the gold leaf to the statues.

The crosier of St. Louis of Toulouse and the cross, held by St. Bonaventure, were made by Monastery volunteer Simon Young, shown here with them.

The Sculptors' Stories

After almost 17 years the Saints were home again. Once the statues had been installed in the two containers, the experts had their first proper opportunity to assess the damage and the amount of work needed to bring them back to their former glory.

Internationally respected artist and sculptor Shawn Williamson already had a working relationship with The Monastery and had worked on early Monastery community arts projects with young offenders and school refusers. His experience in heritage restoration projects and his talent for producing original pieces made him a huge asset to the saints' restoration team.

"When I first saw the statues I thought they were in a bad way," he said. "They'd been knocked about quite a bit, but there was a good chance that they could be salvaged."

The second skilled sculptor and stonemason in the team was Andrew Scantlebury, who was first introduced to The Monastery by his mother Ilma, who was the then Arts Director. Andrew had also worked as part of The Monastery's outreach programme, leading a large number of community arts projects in Gorton over the years.

He took some of the broken pieces of statue to a local stoneyard to find the best possible match for the French limestone that had first been carved almost 150 years ago. Andrew also started the daunting task of cleaning the statues.

"There was a lot of patchy paint, which had to be very carefully removed. For every part we had to select the right method and judge how fragile the original material was." Initial assessments of the statues revealed that lead-based paints had been used in the past, possibly to 'brighten up' the statues at some point. The team needed to use protective equipment to avoid coming into contact with the toxic materials.

Public access to the containers also had to be restricted. Each of the 8ft tall statues weighs over a half a ton, so they were secured to the ceiling of the containers by strong webbing straps, but the danger of one being knocked over and causing injury could never be underestimated. However everyone involved in bringing the Saints home felt it was critical that members of the public should be given the chance to see them up close.

The sculptors worked on the statues and the containers were open for public viewing on all of The Monastery's regular Open Sundays. It really was a unique opportunity to see the incredible crafts-manship and one that will never be possible again, now that the saints are back in their original positions in the Great Nave.

Angela Colley was a volunteer who worked alongside Andrew. "There was a lot of cleaning to do, even after the paint was removed. It was the remains of old pollution and old heating etc, plus the saints were handled quite a lot after they were taken out of

the church. As soon as we put water on them it turned to mud. We just used a simple soap and water solution, then worked up from a gentle sponge, through brushes of different hardness, depending on how dirty they were. Parts were very delicate so we just had to be patient and take our time."

The restoration work itself called upon a range of skills from the two sculptors. Shawn said, "We had to work in the original style of the original sculptors. After you start working with the stone and observing the work, you get an instinct for how to proceed." Shawn's preferred method for replacing missing parts is to work directly in stone. "You cut back into the original piece and use special steel dowels to anchor the new pieces. You cut both parts with oblique angles for a better fix."

One of his favourite parts of the job was replacing St. Clare's missing nose. "The nose was broken off and the stone was very worn away. I carved a nose, which was then matched in and then I carved again to bring it all together."

"The statues were designed to be viewed from the ground, not from in front," he continued. "If you look at her lips, they protrude a lot, but that's just part of the exaggeration of the features so that they can be seen clearly from the ground. Her nose had to be shaped to work with that."

Heritage restoration is always tricky, but Shawn found adding Saint Leonard's cross one of the biggest challenges. "I really had to cut back a lot and put big dowels in his hand so we could get a really strong fix for the new carving."

Andrew took a slightly different approach to recreating missing parts. "I like to model the features in air-drying clay, directly on the statues, to get the right expression and scale. Then I use these to carve the new stone pieces."

Over the decades before they were removed, some of the statues had been photographed in-situ many times, and several photographs still exist. However these had limited use for artistic reference as the statues were so high in the nave of the church that many of the details were impossible to see. While they were useful for identifying what was actually missing, the two sculptors had to draw on their own experience and tune into the style and scale of the remaining original pieces in order to decide on the level of detail for the new parts.

Once the sculptors had finished, the final stage of the restoration was to gild parts of each statue, highlighting important details to create a bright focus for each one. Terry Colley, the gilder explained, "For some of the statues it was obvious which parts needed to be gold, like the crown of St. Louis IX. However it was important not to put too much on. The Franciscan vow of poverty meant that some of them really shouldn't have much gold, but we didn't want some outshining the others." He felt that in the end, a good balance between the aesthetic and religious influences was reached.

Terry had to wait until all the dust had settled from the stone carving, then several coats of sealant were applied to each statue to seal the porous material, before size was applied, then finally the 23 carat gold leaf.

Working on the saints has been a rewarding experience for everyone involved. Before embarking on the restoration, Shawn had said, "I always remember seeing the saints statues locked away in a container a long time ago. I dreamt that one day they would wake from their sleep. To be part of that awakening and to restore them back to The Monastery is a dream come true." At the end of the project he reflected, "Working in stone is itself almost a spiritual thing – stone has a spiritual dimension. Some of the minerals found in stone also make up our own human bodies. These 'bodies' will outlast us all."

Andrew said, "It has been a challenging project, but it's been great. I would love to do it all over again. In some ways it's a shame it has come to an end, but I'll be immensely happy and proud to see the saints back where they belong."

Clare Mount
June, 2012

Chapter Four

Return

The final part of the journey of the saints was to be both the most challenging, and potentially the most dangerous.

After removing the saints from the container they were placed on specially made pallets and had a crate built around them, to protect them on the journey back into the church.

Bars were placed at strategic points to stop the statues moving around as they were carried.

Left: the crate for Saint Clare being built outside the Monastery while next in line is St. Peter of Alcantara.

To avoid causing problems with traffic on the road outside, the saints are carried around the back of the friary, and in through the front doors. Above: a fork-lift truck with the statue of St. Peter. Below: that of Saint Didacus is entering the church ready to be stored over the weekend.

Once the statues were all back inside the Monastery, the work of Speedy Services was complete. The job of raising the saints up to their original plinths above the pillars in the church, was to be undertaken by Killelea and Anelays. The group pictures show the teams from Speedy Services (above) and Killelea and Anelays (below).

The saints had stood on their plinths for over 100 years without any means of attachment, but modern safety concerns dictated this was no longer permissible. Instead, a rebate was cut into the back of each saint and a hook and wire inserted, which could then be attached to two eyelets placed into the wall behind each statue. Also, a hole was drilled into the base of the statue so it could be fitted over a dowel embedded into the plinth. These measures should, hopefully, hold the saints in their positions for at least the next 100 years.

Here the statue of Saint Elizabeth is being padded with foam to act as a cushion where the lifting straps come into contact with the stone. The straps were then hooked on to the crane so the statue could be lifted to a position slightly above the plinth where it was to stand.

The statue was lowered and guided to fit neatly onto the pin that had been drilled into the plinth. Once it was safely set down the straps were unhooked from the crane and removed. Below left, the straps are removed from Saint Elizabeth of Hungary.

St Louis, pictured right, is being bedded in. After the straps are removed the holding cable will be attached to the eyelets in the wall.

The preaching cross, made by Terry Colley for the statue of Saint Peter of Alcantara, is here being fitted into place. To ensure it does not shift or fall, it was glued into position. You can see the glue being applied in the picture below.

Left: The new cross for Saint Bonaventure was made in two pieces. Here the lower shaft is being threaded up through the statue's hand, so it can be attached to the top section. Quite a difficult operation when standing 40ft high in the cradle of a cherry picker!

Once the two pieces of the cross were attached, and its final angle adjusted, it was glued to the statue's hand.

This statue stands directly above where the pulpit used to be, and if you look closely above the cross, you can see the bracket from which the pulpit's sound board used to hang.

St. Anthony carries a book, upon which rests Christ as a child and he also carries a lily, representing purity. This picture, right, shows the lily resting on his shoulder. It has been finished in gold leaf by Terry Colley.

The pictures below show the men checking exactly how the lily should lie. As with the crosses the lily is placed carefully on the statue and then glued in place.

These pictures show the crosier being fitted on the statue of Saint Louis of Toulouse. Made from wood by Simon Young, and gilded by Terry Colley, it is about 7ft tall and was copied from the few photographs we could find showing the original statue.

The statue of Saint Louis of Toulouse has some fine gilding on his mitre as well as that on the crosier.

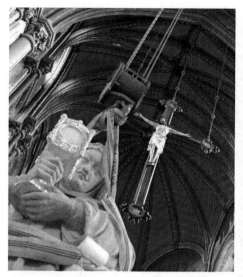

Saint Clare was one of the last of the saints to be raised into position. The two pictures above show her statue being lifted and guided onto the plinth. When it is safely in place, and the straps are removed from the crane, she appears to smile directly at the workmen in a gesture of thanks.

The magnificent saints are all now back in their places above the columns, and another chapter in the restoration of the Monastery is complete.

Chapter 5

Reprise

The Story of *Spirit of Love*

The Monastery at Gorton was built on hope and trust. The architect Pugin, the Franciscan brothers, the builders, stonemasons, sculptors and the many skilled and unskilled workers and helpers from the local community, all hoped and believed that they were creating something truly special. Their labours would produce an enduring legacy that was a testament to the Franciscan values – humility, generosity, reverence, service, respect, prayer, joy and most of all, love.

Gorton Monastery fulfilled their ambition and became a monumental landmark of bewitching, soaring beauty. It demanded the attention of the whole city, acting like a beacon to transmit the guiding principles of the Franciscan Order.

The subsequent story of the dereliction and jubilant re-birth is a remarkable one, but a building, however beautiful, is still just an empty shell. It is the people who use it and the intention of how to use it that fills it with life and love and gives it true meaning.

The Monastery Trust was committed to the continuation of the original Franciscan values, and having restored its awe-inspiring buildings, re-opened in 2007 and offered them to the community, in the spirit of love.

In 2004, the Trust had been approached by refugee Osman Caka, who, together with his family had fled war-torn Kosovo following the murder of his 17 year old son Ilir at the hands of ethnic cleansers. Osman could have responded in so many ways to this deep personal tragedy. He could have tried to seek revenge, or turned with hatred against all Christians, or wallowed in self-pity. Instead he wanted to create something beautiful, an object to say: Love and only love is able to overcome tragedy.

His overwhelming wish was to erect a sculpture, somewhere in his newly-adopted country, to the Albanian born Mother Teresa. As a Christian woman, born in a Muslim country, and who worked chiefly among Hindus, she was revered and respected by all as a wonderful symbol of religious tolerance.

Her inspiration, of how we are all united by our common humanity, and through love can rise above the divisions created by religion, ethnicity, colour and creed, resonated with the Trust, and its belief that the Monastery should serve the community in the same way, being open to all.

The Monastery's chief executive, Elaine Griffiths, was very moved by the proposed idea. "There are many parallels between Osman's personal story of tragedy and our 10 year struggle to rescue this once much-loved church. The building, now beautifully restored, is again a focal point for the community, welcoming all that come here, regardless of differences of faith, creed or ethnic background."

One can only imagine how the Franciscans who built the Monastery might have reacted to this moving story and remarkable man. Osman's decision to overcome his personal tragedy was to instigate the creation of something meaningful and beautiful, a reminder to all that love and forgiveness are the way forward.

In order to progress the project, the Trust invited submissions of ideas on the theme of The Spirit of Love, while fundraising also began.

One that was received, the design of a young Manchester-based artist, Andrew Scantlebury, stood out. Trained as a stonemason, he has a degree in Fine Art from Salford University, specialising in sculpture. As an enthusiastic supporter of the Monastery, he had been involved with the project for over 10 years and had led numerous training events for the Trust, involving local schools, youth clubs and the general public.

His love of the Monastery buildings and deep understanding of the Trust's aims led him to create a proposal rich with meaning, expressing beautifully what the newly renovated Monastery stands for.

Andrew suggested a 2m tall abstract work in white Portland stone, to echo the French limestone of the High Altar inside the Monastery's Great Nave. His chosen work is based on two hands, pointing upwards, as in prayer or supplication, gently encircling and protecting a rounded egg-like shape within them. He also took plaster casts of Mrs Caka's hands, using them to guide the eventual design, linking the concept to the family that had originally inspired it.

Having finished the sculpture, Andrew said, "To complete this project this year (2007) is particularly poignant because it is not only the year the Monastery building finally re-opened, but it is also the tenth anniversary of Mother Teresa's death." He continued, "This work was a real labour of love. It's a very personal statement. Osman wanted to create something truly thought-provoking, not just as a memorial to his son, but as a statement about humanity and how we should live our lives. Thanks to him, something beautiful has come from this tragedy. It is a great honour to have played a part in this project."

The sculpture is an overall arched shape, harmonising with the gothic windows and doors of the buildings. The rounded, almost pregnant form, symbolises new life, a new beginning and gentle protection, just as Mother Teresa cared for her people.

The Spirit of Love now stands at the front of the Monastery, facing out onto Gorton Lane. It was unveiled on 31st August 2007, on the tenth anniversary of Mother Teresa's death, attended by the Bishop of Kosovo, the Minister of Culture for Macedonia and many leading figures for all the major faiths in Manchester. It was funded entirely by donations from local businesses and individuals*.

Its originator, Osman Caka was delighted to see the completed work and said, "I believe love and only love is able to overcome tragedy. It is wonderful to see the statue in such a prominent place in front of this beautiful building. Andrew has created something quite remarkable and wonderful." Looking to the future he added, "My wish is that this piece of art be a constant reminder for future generations, that we should all live side by side in peace and harmony. May The Spirit of Love stand for tolerance and love for all."

*Sponsors included: Mother Teresa, Humanitarian Charitable Society of Switzerland (Pjeter Gjoni, President); Exclusafe Ltd, Urmston (Mr and Mrs Moulton); A.R. Stocktons and Co. Ltd, (Mr Stockton); AMTEC Ltd; Rawwater Ltd; GATE LLC; ACM Instruments; Mrs Moilio Regan; Ms Adetutu Fapohunda; and others who wished to remain anonymous.

Ilma Scantlebury and Clare Mount

June 2012

Chapter Six

Our Continuing Story

The Trust has achieved a great deal since it was formed in 1996 but there is still so much more to do.

In this 150th Anniversary year the Trust is launching another fundraising campaign in order to fulfil its original vision for The Monastery. We hope to build on the project's success so far and on its status as an award winning venue and heritage regeneration exemplar.

It is also our intention to ensure that the unique position that the Monastery holds in the heart of the community is secured for the future generations to enjoy and experience.

The Trust will be making a new application for funding support to the Heritage Lottery Fund and other grant making trusts. Our 150th Anniversary Appeal hopes to raise enough money through donations and matched funding to deliver the following projects and opportunities in partnership with our existing partners and stakeholders;

Charitable, Heritage Education and Community Projects

- To further develop our community projects and support charitable work in the local community including Gorton Voice Choir and Gorton Visual Arts Group.
- To further develop the heritage tours, talks and educational programmes to reach a wide audience of young people and senior citizens alike through groups, societies, universities, colleges, schools and community groups.

- To share the story of the Monastery's rich historical, spiritual, cultural and architectural journey with as many visitors as possible.
- To provide heritage information, support materials and resources through exhibition and display materials, through Monastery publications and DVDs and through the development of digital aids such as a Monastery App and the launch of a new website.

Restoration and Conservation projects

- To continue the restoration process of the building to ensure the preservation of its heritage for the benefit of future generations and International visitors who conference in the City.

- To restore and repair the Lady Altar to develop a permanent discreet area for all faiths, backgrounds and beliefs to use for peace, contemplation, prayer and quiet reflection.

- Commission and create a Saint Francis Sculpture on site as part of a community based heritage training project for young people.

- Commission and create a permanent Labyrinth in the grounds of the Monastery as part of a community based arts & health project.

- To restore the original Pugin stencils and paint schemes therefore preserving an important part of the architectural and heritage story of The Monastery.

- To repair and partially restore the High Altar.

- To rectify water damage to chancel walls and damage to the original Victorian tiled floor.

- To install a scaffolding rig so there is permanent and safe access to the roof space for on-going maintenance of the heritage asset.

Improving the Visitor, Conference & Venue Facilities

- To improve the visitor experience and facilitate the event and conference spaces with the development of a permanent front wing.

- It will be designed to provide a sustainable and flexible hospitality function and will include new washroom facilities with a reception and gift shop space.

- The space will also provide opportunity to install interpretation exhibition materials to tell the story of the Monastery.

The Sustainable Showcase and the Monastery Village Development

- The building will also help to fulfil an aspiration for The Monastery to act as an exemplar for sustainability.

- The core values of sustainability, community involvement, education and engagement are central to the Monastery's philosophy.

- The Monastery is in discussions with UNESCO and is bidding with partners to become one of the key sites in Greater Manchester that will become a Regional Centre of Expertise (RCE) for education in sustainable development.

- To ensure this becomes an active part of the future work of the Monastery, sustainability principles will be embedded into the design of all new build spaces so that it can act as an exemplar for the local community and education programmes in the local area.

Also sitting centrally to this project is the requirement to consider the connectivity of the Monastery with the City and the wider region. This connection can be considered physically through heritage of the building and the public realm and intellectually through the interpretation of its heritage. Of equal importance is the religious and social context. This can be explored further through the recent discoveries around the architecture, spirituality and sacred geometry alongside the Franciscan narrative that already exists.

The Monastery site and its buildings do not stand in isolation. It is vital that they are allowed to contribute fully to the City and the wider national monastic, cultural, artistic, architectural and religious heritage. The quality of heritage on this site has the potential to deliver a world class story.

On the next page: Trust Chief Executive Elaine Griffiths discusses future plans for the Monastery with HRH The Prince of Wales during his recent visit.

'The Prince's Foundation for Building Community' is helping the Trust with their sustainability plans for the Monastery village.

Acknowledgements

In the early years of the project, when the Monastery was still in ruins, we created our *Save a Saint, Adopt an Angel and Buy a Brick* ideas for fundraising and we were successful in generating a great deal of interest and support.

The thought of restoring the precious statues of the Saints and the delicate stonework of the many angels carved around the Monastery Nave was very much a dream for the future. Actually buying bricks was probably closest to reality as we would need tens of thousands of bricks as well as cash donations to raise the millions of pounds that would be needed to save the derelict Monastery. Every penny that we raised had to be diverted to the main purpose of saving and restoring the building. All of those early donations were essential to the project as they would count as matched funding for the large heritage grants that we were hoping to raise from the Heritage Lottery Fund, English Heritage, The North West Development Agency and from European funding and other grant making trusts.

It was a very long and difficult process and eventually we succeeded in raising the £6.5 million needed to save the derelict Monastery and over time it was lovingly restored to become the magnificent multipurpose venue you see today.

We were all aware that all of our generous donors would one day expect to visit the Monastery and see that their donations had been used not only for the bricks in the friary but also to restore and return the 12 saints to their rightful places on their plinths. This would be a very long and complex project on the very long list of possible future projects. For the past few years the 'Return of the Saints' project seemed to move onto the 'too difficult to do' list that had to be put on hold to wait for another more suitable time.

The turning point was 2011 – it was a very difficult time emotionally for all of the Monastery team as we lost our very dear friend and colleague Tony Hurley after a short but fierce battle with cancer. Tony had always been keen to bring the saints back home for the Monastery's 150th Anniversary. Tony always wanted to lead the project as, along with Janet Wallwork, they were our experts on the saints. It felt really important to bring them back to Gorton in Tony's memory during 2011.

How on earth could we possibly achieve that when there was no extra money available?

Just then, a little bit of Monastery magic kicked in.

Speedy plc held their All Stars Awards evening at the Monastery which was a great success. Steve Corcoran, Speedy's Chief Executive and Simon Richards their Executive Support Director offered to help us with the Monastery project if there was ever anything we needed. This was the breakthrough we had been waiting for. Suddenly we had an offer of help from experts in the technical field who had exactly the right equipment and vehicles for the job. They would also know just how to move our precious saints from the Hooper Street City Council Depot in Ardwick safely back to Gorton.

Of course this was not going to be an easy task. We would also need lifting and specialist equipment as well as somewhere on site where we could create workshops for the sculptors with lighting and power for their cutting tools for at least six months or even a year. This was a very big request of any sponsor and remarkably Speedy delivered on all of it.

Speedy Services very kindly brought in their national team of experts to plan, manage and deliver the project. They worked tirelessly and professionally in all weathers alongside Eraina Smith and the city council team at Hooper Street Depot until all of the saints were safely back home on site here at the Monastery.

Speedy also helped to persuade colleagues from Elliotts to provide us with two full size temporary workshops so there was enough room to restore six saints in each container. These workshops were lockable and secure so the saints would be safe and protected for as long as the fundraising and the restoration would take.

Commitment and support from all of our 'saints' team has been above and beyond all of our expectations. It has been the catalyst for everything else to fall into place. We are so grateful for the lifting and hosting expertise provided by Bob Killelea and Gerry Anderson from Killelea & Sons. We are also indebted to Wm Anelay's for their heritage conservation and fixing skills working alongside the structural engineering and loading advice kindly provided by Atkins.

Gold leaf has been generously sponsored by Clive and Dee Stonehouse from Wright's of Lymm. They have also provided us with the services of professional gilder Terry Colley, who has skilfully added the finishing touches.

Our sculptors Andrew Scantlebury and Shawn Williamson started the restoration work together in October 2011. The work continued throughout the winter months as the sculptors ensured that our saints were repaired and had all of the damaged stonework and missing limbs replaced. Work intensified in the past couple of months so that the project could be completed in early June.

Our sculptors have been helped by our regular volunteers who have painstakingly been chipping off the old damaged paint, cleaning the statues and helping with all the general restoration jobs. Special thanks also go to Christine Linaker, Wendy Hughes, Cath Barningham, Louise Kenyon and Angela Colley.

The saints would never have been rescued in the first place without the intervention and determination of Janet Wallwork, helped by Sir Gerald Kaufman and Professor Ted Kitchen, with the support of Manchester City Council.

From the day that the saints were withdrawn from the Sotheby's sale Janet has continued to work tirelessly on behalf of the saints and the Monastery project in her role as Trustee. Janet is currently editing this book on the 'Return of the Saints'.

Our original and current team along with our Monastery friends and regular volunteers have been as hard working and dedicated as ever with their consistent support of the project. There are so many people who have helped us with our 'Save a Saint' project over the years that it will be an impossible task trying to remember and thank everyone by name. We are so grateful to each and every one of you who has sponsored and supported this historic project and helped us to bring the saints back home in this important 150th Anniversary year.

Elaine Griffiths
June 2012

Paul and Elaine Griffiths with Saint Anthony of Padua.

Editor's Acknowledgements

To put a book of this complexity together, at very short notice, has been a tremendous challenge for all concerned. I wish to thank all our named contributors, of course, but also some of the people whose names are not mentioned in the text. We have to thank Sotheby's for the use of their images from the auction catalogue in which the Saints appeared, Dan Dubowitz for his wonderful photo of the Saints in storage, Ray Hanks for proof-reading the text, and Karl Edginton of *Imagine* for his beautiful cover photograph and design. Most of all, I wish to thank the Monastery's Friend and Volunteer, David Ratcliffe, without whose technical skills, hard work and patience, all these separate elements could never have been brought seamlessly together to produce this book.

Janet Wallwork
Trustee
Monastery of St. Francis and Gorton Trust
June 2012

The editor with her favourite Saint, Clare of Assisi.

SAINTS~SUPPER

SPONSORS LIST

**Saint Anthony
of Padua**

**Saint Elizabeth
of Hungary**
The **co-operative** bank
good with money

**Saint Berard
of Carbio**

Saint Ivo of Brittany

**Saint Bernadine
of Siena**

**Saint Leonard
of Port Maurice**

Saint Bonaventure

St Louis of Toulouse

**Saint Clare
of Assisi**

**St Louis,
King of France**

Saint Didacus

**Saint Peter
of Alcantara**

With special thanks to...